PREACHING AT THE TRUCKSTOP

Homilies on the Way to the Big Bash

Fr. Jim Schmitmeyer

D1523350

In Loving Memory

Alberta Pohl

Fr. Jim Schmitmeyer

Author's Note

This collection of homilies for special occasions includes events from holy days to holidays. Also included are observances peculiar to certain localities and regions such as *Quinceañeras* and the Feast of St. Isidore, the Farmer.

The settings for these homilies reflect years of pastoral service rendered to Catholics in the Texas Panhandle, the majority of which are rural communities comprised of both Anglo and Hispanic members.

The names in this book have been altered with the exception of the last homily which was delivered at the funeral of my sister, Alberta.

LOVE'S TRUCK STOP

Introduction

Have you ever walked into a convenience store and found yourself reaching for a holy water font? Of course not. Yet, according to mystic and doctor of the Church, St. Catherine of Siena, such a reaction would not be inappropriate. She was firmly convinced that life is a road trip to Heaven and that the Church serves as a roadhouse to refresh travelers on the way to that ultimate destination.

Hello, my name is Catherine. Would you like fries with that order?

For this preacher, Catherine's insight has proven solid teaching time and again. I recall, for instance, gassing up at a convenience store the week before Father's Day. A working man and his young son pulled up to the air pump. They stepped out of the cab. The boy looked a lot like his dad. My tank was full and, suddenly, so was my soul. That passing experience at a gas station would anchor the words I preached on Father's Day.

Like the wind, the God's Spirit sweeps across the land and cities, carving canyons of meaning and hope in the hard granite of human life.

Do you need a receipt?

Catherine's intuition about the Church as a roadhouse dispensing sacramental nourishment suggests that today's truck stops and rest-stops are more than simply places to stretch our legs, slide into plastic chairs and eat food from a cardboard container. Beneath these desultory activities, a hungry heart encounters nourishment for the soul, a brief respite to contemplate our welcome at the door of the Father's House while surveying bottles of soft drinks, racks of candy bars, and glancing at the disparate folks in line at the counter.

Sorry. That restroom is out of order.

If a person believes in the Incarnation of God in the person of Jesus Christ, the co-mingling of the sacred with the profane provides fertile soil for contemplation and communion, as attested in the oft quoted line from Gerard Manley Hopkins: "God plays in a thousand places." Even those who do not believe in God acknowledge this spiritual dimension of life when they refer to events like a wedding, a hike in the mountains or the birth of a child as something significant and worthy of reverence. What others call a road trip, Christians call a pilgrimage. What others deem significant, Catholics call sacramental.

The experience of two distraught disciples on the road to Emmaus recalls the power of those moments when ordinary routines are pieced by extraordinary revelations.

He broke the bread, and immediately they recognized him.

One does not need to travel to Emmaus to access some dimension of that sacramental encounter. Have you ever noticed the gaze in the eyes of a mother watching her daughter, her youngest, cross a platform on a stage to receive her diploma? Have you savored the aroma of a charcoal fire at a family gathering on the Fourth of July? Have you sung, loud and full-throated, a favorite hymn at a Mass where your grandchild was serving at the altar? Have you wept as you passed rosary beads from finger to finger at the wake of a friend?

These occasions, whether inside a church, on a beach or in a neighbor's backyard, are the roadhouses to which St. Catherine referred: rest-stops where the fever of life stills and we savor a premonition of the eternal Sabbath. *Preaching at the Truck Stop: Homilies on the Way to the Big Bash* is a collection of meditations centered on such places and events: Baptisms, *Quinceañeras*, Holy Week liturgies, Funerals and Weddings, Baccalaureates and Prison Retreats.

I hope these homilies carry something of the wind of the Spirit, sculpting for you canyons of grace along the roads that you travel and the trails that you hike.

The banquet is ready. Come to the feast!

TAG-ALONG

Father's Day

It was about 10 AM when I pulled into Toot-n-Totum to gas up my truck.
Not many customers.
>When I topped off my tank,
>I noticed a black pickup pull up to the air pump.

>It was work truck.
>The paint was faded.
>One fender was coated in primer.
>The tailgate carried a good-sized dent.

But what caught my attention more than the truck itself
was the fact that the driver, a working man,
had his son with him, seven or eight years old.

>They had the same build. The same walk.
>They both wore caps, tee-shirts and faded jeans.
>Clearly, this apple did not fall far from the tree!

>And I thought to myself,
>*What a lucky kid,*
>*tagging along on the job*
>*with his dad on a summer day.*

>I watched them pull away
>and wished I could have chatted with the fellow a few minutes,
>just to learn a bit about their story.

I love stories about fathers.

When I was a kid, my favorite TV show was *The Rifleman*,
a story about a man and his young son living in a cabin,
living off the land, making it on their own.

Sometimes, I wonder what sort of father I would have been if fatherhood had been my calling.

This weekend is Fathers' Day.

Unfortunately, our entertainment industry doesn't focus much on fatherhood.

Fr. Jim Schmitmeyer

Even here, in church, we don't talk much about fathers.
Most of our male saints are priests, bishops and monks.

Yet, we cannot overlook the contribution of fathers.
St. John Paul II once wrote that every effort must be made
"to restore the conviction that the work of the father
in and for the family is unique and irreplaceable."

Today, we thank God for the strength and love
reflected in the fathers we know and admire.

Myself, I'm going to remember the man pumping air into truck tire at Toot-n-Totum.

I don't know his story.
I don't even know if he is a Christian.
But I'm going to pray for him.

I'm going to pray for him because he is a father.
Mainly, I'm praying for him because,
when he knelt to put air in his tire,
his son stood next him with his hand on his shoulder.

I don't know their story.
But I do know God's story.
  A story about a Father who loved his Son.
  The story about a Father who loves us all.

GOD'S MOUNTAIN

Wedding

Ever meet anyone who is happy? *Really, really* happy?

> I'm not talking happy
> because they won the lottery.
> I don't mean happy
> because they have a hundred "likes" on Facebook.

> I am referring to someone who is happy
> deep down inside,
> happy from the inside out.

Just last month, a writer for the *New York Times,* David Brooks,
published a book called *The Second Mountain.*

In this book, he notes that everyone wants to be happy.
In his view, most people set off climbing the mountain of performance and success
in hopes of finding the happiness they seek.
> He calls this the First Mountain.
> Folks who hike the trails of this mountain
> think that happiness will be found
> in making a mark on the world,
> cultivating their talents,
> and living their dreams.
> People on this mountain
> are concerned about their reputations.
> They tend to keep score
> and spend a lot of time wondering,
> "How am I measuring up?"
> They focus on things like a nice home,
> nice vacations
> good food,
> and good friends.

Unfortunately, when they reach the top of that first mountain they don't find happiness, but disappointment.
> Eventually, they wind up back down to the valley

and there, in the valley, they realize
there is a another mountain to climb.
A Second Mountain.

Not the mountain of success and achievement.
But the mountain of self-giving and self-sacrifice.

Now and then, you come across people
who are able to look ahead
and manage to choose to climb the Second Mountain,
the more important mountain, first.

These people,
the ones on the Second Mountain,
are the happy ones.

They are happy "from the inside out."
One reason they are happy in this way
is because they aren't trying to be happy.

This is how Mr. Brooks describes people who are climbing the Second Mountain:

> *They are kind, generous,*
> *delighted by small pleasures and are grateful for large ones.*
> *They are not perfect.*
> *They get exhausted and make errors in judgment.*
>
> *But they live for others, not for themselves.*
> *They know why they were put on this earth*
> *and derive deep satisfaction from doing*
> *what they've been called to do.*
>
> *Life isn't easy for these people.*
> *They've taken on the burdens of others.*
> *Yet they have a serenity about them.*
> *They are not obsessed about themselves,*
> *but have given themselves away.*

They have given themselves away.

Have you met people like this?

A couple of nights ago, I ate supper with Stephanie and Abel.
I couldn't help but notice how happy they were.
Not because they won the lottery...
but because they had found someone
which whom to climb the mountain.
Not their mountain,
but God's mountain.

In short, they know
"why they've been put on this earth;"
their hearts are set
"on doing what they've been called to do."

And what might that be?
What it is, exactly, that Abel and Stephanie have been called to do?

To learn the answer, ask the two of them.
All you need to do is ask them.

If you ask Abel, for instance, he will tell you,
as he told me that night at supper,
that it is all about *God's plan*.

Those are *his* words, not mine.

> When I asked Abel and Stephanie
> why they had chosen these Scripture readings
> about the creation of man and woman,
> Abel said,
> "God has a plan.
> He created man. He created woman.
> God has a plan.
> It's our job to live according to his plan."
>
> That's what he said.
> But note what he did not say.
> He didn't say, "Life is about living our dream."
> He said, "Life is about living God's plan."

I sat back and thought to myself,
"This guy's a mountain climber!
And he's not climbing his own mountain,
he's climbing God's mountain!"

I then asked Stephanie
about the readings they had chosen for their wedding Mass.
> She thought for a moment,
> then said that she really valued the words of St. Paul
> in the second reading,
> words that describe the love that lies
> at the heart of God's plan for a married couple:
> "Love is patient, love is kind.
> Love is not self-serving, it does not insist on its own way.
> Rather, love rejoices in the truth.
> It bears all things. Believes all things. Hopes all things.

Endures all things.
Love never fails."

Then she smiled and repeated what Abel had already said.
"Our love for each other is a part of God's plan."

And I thought to myself,
"Stephanie is happy. She is so happy!
Happy from the inside out!"

And we, ourselves, are happy for the two of them!
We are happy and privileged to be here today,
this day when Abel and Stephanie, "give themselves away."
In good times and in bad,
in sickness and in health...

Today, they give themselves away.
They give their lives away ...to each other...
according to the plan of God.

How noble is that?

And what does God's plan for them look like?
What does it entail?

If you think you do not know,
if you think you have no clue about what God's plan holds for them
—or what His plan holds for you—
you are mistaken.

Because "The Plan," you see,
was set in place long ago,
before the beginning of time.

We *all* know God's Plan,
We *all* know how it will play out.
Because *all* we have to do
is take a good look at Abel and Stephanie.

We have only to look at the family love
in which Stephanie and Abel were raised
and the Catholic faith in which they were formed,
this training in the work of love
which has brought them to this day
in which they give themselves away...

into the arms of each other
and into the arms of Christ.

This is the Plan of God.
God's Plan is the path of genuine love that counts no cost.
     The love that give itself away...
     by putting in an honest day's work
     at the grain elevator and the mechanic shop,
     feeding steers and milking cows and leading a 4-H club;
     teaching catechism at your parish church
     and volunteering as a firefighter for you hometown;
     being humble and kind and strong in character;
     giving thanks to God for daily bread
     giving praise to God for resilience in the hard times
     and contentment in the good times...

     In doing these things with confidence and faith,
     Abel and Stephanie are already living the plan that God has for them.

What a wonderful plan it is

And what a wonderful view it affords!
The breath-taking view that awaits them, someday,
from the top of the mountain.
     The summit of the mountain.
     That glorious mountain.
     The glorious mountain of God.

MANY COLORS

Funeral

At times like this, when words fail us,
what do we do?

Well, we do what the friends of Tabitha did back in the days of the Bible:
We cry.
We shed tears.
We gasp for breath.

> When Peter arrived at the home of Tabitha,
> that is exactly what he encountered:
> her friends and relatives, crying, overcome with grief.

> Then, after they composed themselves,
> they did something else,
> something touching,
> something very human.
> Because Tabitha was a seamstress,
> they brought out some of the garment that she had sewn.

> And then, I suspect, they cried some more
> as they showed St. Peter
> the fine fabric, the expert stitching, delicate embroidery.

Why did they do this?

> Because they wanted Peter to know that her life,
> her wonderful life...resembled a quilt,
> a beautiful quilt.

> All of its pieces put together in such a way
> that they formed an intricate pattern of grace and love.

A few days ago,
when I visited with some members of Martha's family,
they mentioned that one of her favorite things to do was crochet.

And they shared some of the wonderful ways in which her love
kept her family knitted together...

gentle as the yarn of an afghan…
as colorful as the patterns on a doily.

For Martha, her family was everything.
And she was everything to them.

When words could not convey the depth of her love,
Martha was quick to employ hugs and kisses
to say what her words could not express.

She was their rock.

The love and support that we see in her family today,
the support shown by all of you here at this Mass,
all this is a testimony to the love that Martha carried in her heart.
But it is also more than that.

It is a testimony to the power of faith,
faith in God whose love is stronger than death,
whose promises reach far beyond what you and I can imagine.

It was here, in this church,
that Martha made her profession of faith this past spring.
It was here where she sang praise to the Holy Trinity.
It was here where she heard the Word of God and
and found a seat reserved for her at the table of the Lord.

It is here, in this church, where you and I gather today.
And, like the friends of Tabitha,
we hold the many pieces of Martha's life in our hands
and we present them to the Lord.

With sorrow in our hearts
but hope in our eyes…we look to him, who once said,

"I am the Good Shepherd.
I lose not one of those whom the Father has given me."

Today, with trust and faith in the Good Shepherd,
we place the quilt of Martha's life---
its bright colors,
its gentle softness,
its enfolding warmth…
we place her life,
we commend her soul
into His hands, the hands of the Shepherd
who knows His sheep
and calls them each by name.

RANCH RODEO

The Feast of All Saints

Next weekend, the City of Amarillo
will host the National Finals Ranch Rodeo.

> Here in Texas,
> we know the difference
> between Professional Rodeo and Ranch Rodeo.

> Professional Rodeo
> is comprised of individuals competing
> against other individuals.

> Ranch rodeo, on the other hand,
> is more like football:
> a team of cowboys
> (not the Dallas Cowboys, but actual cowboys)
> from one ranch
> compete against teams of cowboys
> from other ranches.

This Sunday, some of us will be at the Ranch Rodeo Finals.
But today, we gather to celebrate the Feast of All Saints,
a feast that reminds us that,
as members of the Church,
we are members of a team.

Just as ranch rodeo differs from professional rodeo,
by being a team sport,
today's feast differs, in a fundamental way,
from the feasts of individual saints.

For instance, today is not the Feast of St. Francis (when we bless animals).
> It is not the Feast of St. Blaise (when we bless throats).
> It is not the Feast of St. Joseph (when we bless bread).

> Today is not the Feast of St. Mother Teresa
> Today is not the Feast of St. John Paul II.

> Rather, the saints we honor today

are those whose names do *not* appear
in that Hall of Fame that we call the Calendar of Saints.

Rather, the saints for whom we give thanks to God today
are known and remembered by relatively few people...
usually just family members and good friends.

Yet, they are honored and loved by God
no less than those amazing, canonized saints
known by all the world.

You know the saints whom I'm talking about:

Your grandmother.
Your favorite uncle who helped you get your first job.
The Sister of St. Francis who prepared you for First Communion.
The older brother whom you loved, who went to war,
and never came home.

This is their feast. The Feast of All Saints.
But not just their feast.
It is our feast as well.
Why?
Because Christianity is a team sport, not individual competition.

St. Paul often used examples from the world of sports
to talk about life in Christ and life within His Church.

His word for "sin," for instance,
was an athletic term from the sport of archery.
It meant "missing the mark," as in "missing the bull's eye."

St. Paul also acknowledged the value of teamwork
and team spirit.
He especially liked using the word "encouragement."
Every one of his letters begins with words of encouragement.

Always, he *encouraged* Christians
to *encourage* one another.

In my opinion, the best image we can conjure in our minds

of the exhilarating grace that infuses this Feast of All Saints,
is a sports stadium packed full with...*saints*!

Imagine that scene.

> A stadium of saints praying for us!
> Cheering for us!

> Saints *who know you.*
> Yes, I'm talking about your grandmother, your uncle,
> your older brother!

> Saints who love you.
> Saints who crowd along the asphalt track at a marathon
> shouting words of encouragement
> with the finish-line in sight!

> They stand and cheer!
> Smiles on their faces.
> Shouts on their lips.
> Towels in hand to wipe away your sweat.
> Bottles of water to quench your thirst.
> Spurring you on to victory.
> And waiting,
> just waiting to embrace you!
> Just waiting to wrap you in their arms again!

THE GREATEST PRAYER ON EARTH, THE MOST POWERFUL PRAYER IN HEAVEN

Vocation Sunday

Sometimes,
parents talk about peeking through the door
of their children's bedrooms
and gazing on their little ones asleep in their beds.

At that moment, parents know the reason
why God put them on the face of this earth.

A sense of fulfillment floods their hearts.
And that sense of fulfillment is a blessing from God.

What is fulfillment?
It's when our deepest desires and God's deepest desires join together...
and something wonderful results.

> You earn a college degree.
> You open your own beauty shop.
> You buy some ground.
> You build a house.

Who doesn't cherish a sense of fulfillment?

But, you know what the best kind of fulfillment is?
It's when you know that you are helping to make
the world a better place.

> You raise a good family.
> You build a strong marriage.
> That's where it starts.

> Maybe you do a little bit more if and when you can:
> You coach Little League
> You sponsor a child in Africa

These are benchmarks on the road to character.
These are signs that point you in the direction of your truest self.

Fr. Jim Schmitmeyer

These are doors that God opens
to show us the way
to a life of purpose, meaning and fulfillment.

"Jesus disembarked from the boat and saw the crowds
and his heart was moved to pity.
For they were like sheep without a shepherd."

Whenever I read this passage,
I find myself in a cop car at 3 AM in the morning.
It's thirty-some years ago and I'm in Cincinnati
drinking coffee and eating a donut
overlooking the lights of the city.

> I was a seminarian at the time.
> And a part-time chaplain for the Cincinnati Police Department.
> I don't remember the name of the officer behind
> the wheel of the police cruiser,
> but I remember that night
> when we drove to the top of one of the seven hills
> on which the city is built.
>
> We pulled over to gaze on the beautiful lights.
> The quiet streets.
> The houses and apartment buildings down below.
>
> It was winter-time
> and snow was falling
> and the city spread out before us
> as peaceful-looking as a Christmas card.
>
> Yet, my mind could not ignore
> all the pain, all the suffering concealed within the shadows.
> In the alleys.
> In the slums.
> The busted needles.
> The busted-up faces.
> The bruised women.
> The broken lives.

As long as I live, I'll never forget that night.

Because on that night I knew, as I never knew before,
that I was called to be a priest.

In today's gospel,
Jesus' disciples have just returned from their first attempt
to save the world.

He had sent them out
to cure the sick and proclaim the Kingdom of God.
They returned jubilant...but tired
So he said to them,
"Come away with me and rest awhile."

That's what he said to his disciples back then,
and that is what he says to his disciples—that's you and me—here today.

> "Come and rest," says the Lord.
> "The week is over.
> Your work is put-on-hold.
> Now, enter into the Sabbath."

So, parents, take a moment to stand at the bedroom door
and gaze on your children as they sleep.

My friends, take time this weekend, take time on this Sabbath,
to peek through a crack in the office door you closed on Friday.

> Take a moment to gaze on the work that you accomplished
> and the sacrifices you offered
> out of love of Christ and out of love for the people
> whom you carry with you in your heart.

> On the job,
> on over-time.
> At the office, in the kitchen, in the laundry room
> At the doctor's office,
> at the grocery store,
> while waiting in traffic.
> In the truck cab
> In the tractor cab

"Come, gaze on the fruits of your labor this week...

and rest with me," says the Lord.

"Rest at my side…
rest in the knowledge that I accept, receive and appreciate
the work you have done…the sacrifices you have offered in my name."

"Come and rest."

In a short time, here at this Mass,
I receive the gifts that are brought to the altar.
> These gifts are holy.
> "Holy gifts from God's holy people."
> They are holy because they are symbols of who you are,
> the life that you live and the love that you give…
> week after week
> year after year

> Your life, offered on the altar of unconditional love.
> Your life, on the altar of the Cross,
> offered in union with Christ, for the salvation of the world.

Nothing more. Nothing *less!*

Your life, your sweat, your blood,
mingled with that of Christ on the wood of the Cross,
poured out for the salvation of the World.

This is why you are here today.

This is why the Mass
is the greatest prayer on the face of the Earth.
And the most powerful prayer in the Halls of Heaven:

> It is Christ's Prayer.
> It is your prayer.
> It is the offering of all that we are
> and all that we shall be.

GET MAD!

The Feast of Pentecost

I was visiting friends in Kansas a couple years ago.
We attended their son's soccer game.

At halftime, their team was losing.
One of the fathers went to the bench and pulled his son aside.
He grabbed the shoulder, got in the boy's face and he said:
"Son! You got to get mad!! You get out there…and GET *MAD*!"

Karen, my friend's wife was sitting next to me.
She leaned over and said, "That man's our preacher."

"Really?" I replied. "That's not what I'd expect from a preacher."

Today is Pentecost and guess what?
The words we hear in Church today
are not words we normally expect from God.

> Those apostles gathered in fear
> inside that Upper Room in Jerusalem
> certainly did not expect a fireworks display
> with tongues of flame lickin' the air!
>
> They did not expect the blowing dust and banging doors
> of a West Texas wind
> to interrupt their nervous little prayers!
>
> But that is exactly what they got: something they didn't expect.
> And that is what we are experiencing today.
> Something we do not expect.
> Something like God
> grabbing us by the shoulders
> and getting right in our face and yelling:
> "Get Mad! Go out there and pick a fight!"

Why is it, when we speak about prayer
we so often speak of God "whispering to us?"

How easily we forget that, sometimes, God SHOUTS!

I was reminded of this recently

when I read a blog by a guy named Bob Goff.

> He mentioned the young man in Bible named Joshua.
> Again and again, in the book that bears his name,
> God eggs him on: "Be strong! Be courageous!"

> Like that Methodist minister telling his son:
> "Get mad! Go out there and Get MAD!"

Today, God sends us his Spirit.
Among the gifts of the Spirit is fortitude.
What is fortitude?
Fortitude is inner strength that doesn't give up!

We see God imparting that gift in dramatic form
in today's scene in the Upper Room.

> God send fire and wind into the Upper Room
> to drive those disciples down the stairs
> and out into the street.

> Why?
> To pick some fights!

> And they did.
> The Acts of the Apostles mentions the apostles getting arrested
> and thrown into jail
> no less than ten times.

> "Go pick a fight!" says God to the apostles.

> And His message to us today is the same:
> "Get out of this church...
> and *go make a difference!*"

We need this divine shove in the back.
Why?
Because it is a lot easier to pick an opinion
than it is to pick a fight.

> It is easier to pick an organization or a church or a team
> and wave their flag and cheer from the sidelines
> than it is to get out on field.

Why?
> Because picking isn't pretty.
> It's messy
> It's time consuming.
> It's painful.
> It's costly.

It's a honky-tonk bar with shouting, yelling,
and fists-a-cuffs in the parking lot.

Sounds a lot like the Gospel to me!

In my life as a priest,
I've heard many people confess the sin of anger.

Each time, I ask for a clarification.
I ask if their anger was an occasion of sin or an occasion of grace.

Then I remind them that the great saint and theologian, Thomas Aquinas,
advised Christians to get angry more often.

Anger is *not* a sin...not when you are angry
at something that is not right!

This is the reason God urges us today
to get mad and pick a fight.

If something's not right,
we need to pick a fight with what's wrong...
and help our God make it right.

> That's what we're here for.
> That's what our religion is about.

> It's not about making you feel good,
> rather, it's about making the world a better place.

That's what we Catholics pray for
each time we pray the prayer to the Holy Spirit:

You know how it goes:

> *Come, Holy Spirit, fill the hearts of the faithful...*
> *enkindle in them the fire of your love...*
> *and we shall be re-born!*
> *And you shall renew the face the earth.*

> *YOU SHALL RENEW THE FACE OF THE EARTH!*

Pentecost is about helping God
make this world a better place:
So, go and pick a fight!
Leave this church today,
and make this world
a better place.

GOOD HANDS

Funeral

The passage we just heard from the Book of Sirach.
gives honor to people who work with their hands.

> It mentions the farmer
> whose mind is fixed on the furrows that he plows,
> the blacksmith
> whose skin is scorched by the fire in the forge,
> the potter
> who stays up late cleaning the kiln.

> The passage gives recognition
> to workers who depend on their hands for their livelihood
> and rely on God for their strength.

> Without such workers,
> "there would be no cities,
> no traveling far and near."

Today, we might want to add architectural engineers and field project managers
to that list of farmers, blacksmiths and potters.

> Those behind-the-scenes kind of folks
> who know about things like
> bearing weight,
> structural design,
> electrical systems
> HVAC and fire protection.

Our friend, Tom, was that kind of guy.
Humble. Knowledgeable. Reliable. Resilient.

And, like the structures and systems he designed,
there existed deep within him,
out-of-sight,
a stout heart and deep soul.

I'm referring here
to the inner strength of a husband and father

who provided not only stability to his marriage and family,
but joy, happiness and an abiding love as well.

> Tom coached his sons in sports.
> He sketched beautiful drawings for his daughters.
> He helped his neighbors
> and volunteered in the community.

> He loved life.
> He worshipped God.
> He gave all that he had in everything he did.

Where does a person learn how to do this?
How does a person develop this sort of strength and vigor?

At one point in the Gospel, Jesus talks about a man
whose house does not collapse beneath the winds of change
or the storms of life
because it is built on a strong foundation,
that foundation being nothing less than the Word of God,
a Word that is put into practice
through a life of faith, hope and love.

Tom knew this.
He was not hesitant to talk about the need
for strong foundations in a person's life.
> (And one of the ways that he got this point across
> was to let people know that *the best thing he ever did
> in life* was marry Janet!)

Together, Tom and Janet raised a wonderful family.

Tom was deeply and rightfully proud of his children.

> Back in September,
> the entire family gathered at his home
> to celebrate his 83rd birthday.

> It is a day that everyone in his family will remember.
> Among the things that they will remember from that day
> will be Tom's smile.

> His face beaming with happiness.
> His heart brimming with love.

In today's gospel passage,

we heard words about letting go of worry
and placing one's life in God's hands.

Do not worry what you are going to eat, says the Lord.
Don't worry about having clothes to wear.
Your heavenly Father knows you need these things
and He will provide all that you need.

Janet chose this reading
because it reflects the faith of her husband.

And, I'm sure, she wants us all to emulate his faith...
the humble faith we find in people who work behind the scenes
to make this world a good place in which to live.

People like the farmer, the blacksmith, the potter.
People whose hands grow the food we eat,
weave the clothes we wear
and build the shelters we inhabit.

Today, you and I also do something important with our hands:
we raise them in prayer
as we commend Tom's soul
into the hands of Christ.

As we do so, we know that we leave him "in good hands."
The hands of the Carpenter.
Hands that blessed.
Hands that bled.
    Strong hands.
    Gentle hands.
    Very good hands, indeed.

A HOUSE ON THE HILL

The Feast of Our Lady of Guadalupe

Tonight, I have three stories to tell you.
Three stories about three Houses, Three Hills and Three Mothers
All of them are true.

Story Number One:
My friend grew up poor on a small farm in southern Ohio
His parents grew tobacco to make a living.

> One day, he and his mother were cutting tobacco.
> The work is slow and tedious.
> The stalks drip a thick syrup that draws flies and mosquitoes.
>
> His mother pauses and wipes the sweat from her face.
> She points to a hill in the distance.
> "What a beautiful house," she says.
>
> The boy looks at the hill, then at his mother.
> "Are you okay?" he asks.
> "Can't you see it?"
> "Ma, there ain't no house."
> "Oh, yes, there is," she takes a deep breath,
> then leans on her hoe. "Oh yes, son. Yes, there is."

The second story, like the first,
involves a man, a woman and a house on a hill.
The man's name is Juan Diego and the name of the hill is Tepeyac.

> One day, on his way to church,
> a bright light appears at the top of the hill.
> A beautiful woman with brown skin
> speaks to him in his own language.
>
> "I am your mother
> and the mother of all those who call on me.

Build a temple on this hill," she says.
"A house for me and my Son
A beautiful house on this hill of Tepeyac."

The third story, like the story of Juan Diego,
also involves a church on a hill and a woman.

The woman in this story is a Franciscan sister named Mother Carmen.

For many years, Mother Carmen ministered to the people of the state of Chiapas,
one of the poorest regions of Mexico.

I visited her one summer.
She took me to a remote village named Tepeyac.
At the top of a hill,
an abandoned barn had been converted into a chapel.
The roof was tin. The door was green.
A humble shed for the Word of God and the Bread of Angels.

Three stories. Three hills. Three houses.
Three places of hope, beauty and peace.

Where is your "house on a hill?"
Where is your Tepeyac?

Is it not here?
In this church on top of this hill?
On the edge of this town?
Is this not our Tepeyac?

Has not our Mother drawn us here tonight?
To this Temple?
To this house for her and her Son?
Is this not our Tepeyac?

Behold its beauty.
Behold its sanctity.
Behold the hope in the hearts of the children of Mary.
Behold the faith of the people of God.
Behold the joy of the church that gathers at the top of this hill!

LIGHT FOR ALL TO SEE

Wedding

The first time Jacob and Jessica came to my office
for marriage preparation,
I learned that, later that afternoon,
Jacob intended to take Jessica deer hunting.

And I thought to myself:
Love is an amazing thing!

As I prepared this wedding homily,
I thought back to that day.
And I thought about this gospel passage we just heard,
a passage that talks about light coming forth from a lamp...

> And I found myself thinking of Jacob, in a deer blind,
> alone in the morning light, scanning the horizon for a sign of deer.

> Myself, I'm not a hunter, but most of my friends are.
> Now and then, I've heard them admit that the reason they like to hunt,
> isn't so much to hunt...
> but to pray.

Most men find it easiest to pray outdoors.
And, come the fall of the year,
when pheasant season or deer season opens,
there's a type of prayer that occurs
when light illumines the prairie grass
and all is quiet

The prayer of the hunter isn't a prayer that asks God for a good shot at a buck.
It's more than that...
a prayer of praise for the Creator of the world.

The prayer that comes to the lips of a man in the morning light
is a prayer of hope.
> His hope to be a worthy husband for the woman he loves...
> a prayer to be true to his commitments...
> a prayer whispered in that morning light,
> a prayer to walk in the Light of Truth
> and to be the husband that God calls him to be.

There is another kind of prayer
that occurs in the soft gleam of light.
I am referring to the prayer of a wife when,
on a winter night, headlights sweep across the yard and into the drive...
and a woman breathes a sigh of relief
because the husband she loves has made it home safe through a storm.

> So she waits for him
> at the door beneath the light of the porch
> and the snow she cursed an hour ago
> turns soft in the fading light.

> And as they take each other in their arms,
> gratitude enfolds them
> and, at that very moment,
> they realize that the two of them are held in the arms of God,
> arms as strong and ancient as the wind in the trees.

Such is the prayer that rises up in the morning light.
That prayer that is uttered in the evening dusk.
That prayer that is offered when hearts grow warm in the light of love.

"You are the light of the world," says Jesus.
"No one lights a lamp then puts it under a bushel basket.
Rather, it is set on a table where it gives light to all in the house."

In a few moments,
Jacob and Jessica will speak the vows of marriage
before God and the church.

It was God's light that first illumined the nature of their love,
now, their love illumines the nature of God...

For deep within the love they promise to live today
for the rest of their lives...
shines the love of Christ himself.

As soft as the light the makes its way across a field at dawn,
as necessary as headlights on the car that carries you home at the end of the day.

God's love illumines the Sacrament of Matrimony.
The Sacrament of Matrimony illumines the love of God.

This is what we're taught and this is what we know:
> When you look upon a man and woman living the sacrament of marriage,
> you see more than a man and a woman,
> you see more than a marriage.
> you see Christ himself
> the light of his love

here today,
set high a on stand,
giving light to all in the house...
giving light for all to see.

HOMETOWN

Baccalaureate

In a few moments we will be shown a slideshow.
Wonderful, funny, beautiful pictures.
Pictures of you, your classmates, your families, your friends.

On a night like this, pictures are important.

So important are these pictures
that I wish I myself could paint a picture in words
about each one of you,
a picture that would capture, for just a moment,
who you are at this time in your life...

> If I could create such a picture,
> that picture would include
> more than just a reflection of you.

> It would also include
> the hope we hold for each of you,
> the pride we carry in our thoughts of you
> the joy we feel in our souls for you.

Before we view the slideshow,
I ask that each of us here,
especially the graduates,
look closely at the pictures.
And, as you do so,
remember to notice the background of the photos,
not just the foreground.

> When you do this,
> you'll notice that all the backgrounds are all the same.

> It won't matter if the picture's shot
> on the football field,
> at the stock show

in the bleachers,
on the basketball court,
in the study hall;
it wouldn't matter if the shot is taken inside your home
on Christmas day or your birthday;
it won't matter if you happen to be
leading an Angus steer at the stock show,
holding trophy at a regional tournament,
or waving to the camera
as you lean from the window of a car.

The background of each shot
will be nothing less that that which God has provided:
a place and a community called Vega, Texas.

You know, people often talk about how God creates each individual
as a unique, one-in-a-kind person
with his or her own unique DNA, physical features, personality traits, etc.

Something we do not often talk about
is that God also created you
for a unique place.

This unique and special place
plays an important part
in the person you turn out to be.

I'm talking about this town, this land, this community
that has formed your attitudes,
shaped your values,
taught you virtue,
provided a vision of what it means to be human
in the deepest and truest sense.

Graduates, you are a part of us.
We are a part of you.

Now, maybe this isn't something you want to hear.
After all, you are young.
Perhaps you are "chomping at the bit"
to get out of this town.

What young person doesn't want
adventure
excitement
a chance to prove yourself?
This is good and completely understandable.

But...the pictures...these pictures...
the ones with your eyes full of hope and laughter...
the ones that glory in your friends and your family and everyone who loves you...

>   these pictures also contain a certain backdrop:
>   the halls of this school,
>   the pews of your church,
>   the stadium bleachers,
>   the courthouse,
>   the gas station,
>   the grocery store.

>   Your home. Your hometown.
>   Spread out beneath the open sky.
>   Pastures. Corn fields and feedlots.
>   Chiseled canyons as ancient as the wind.
>   And long, empty roads
>   that carry your eyes to the horizon.

The place where we live
forms who we are.

Can you imagine knowing the Lord
without knowing that he was born in Bethlehem?
That he worked as carpenter in Nazareth.

Could you say that you know Him well
without knowing that
>   he confronted Satan in the desert?
>   washed his disciples' feet in the Upper Room?
>   sweated blood in Gethsemane?
>   shoved aside a stone at the entrance of a tomb outside Jerusalem?

Here's my point:
we cannot think of Jesus without thinking of the place he came from.

And the same goes for you!

See this piece a barbed wire?

I own a piece of ground down in Briscoe County.
But somebody else owned that place long before I did.
This wire is Huber Wire from 1882.

This land on which we live carries many stories.
Our lives are episodes within those stories.

> A couple Saturdays ago
> I tagged along with a friend of mine who works in the oil fields.
> Manuel is also a cowboy
> and he knows that land like the back of his hand.
>
> "Over there," he pointed, "you'll find the corner of a stone house
> where Billy the Kid used to hide out."
> He smiled and I thought he was joking.
>
> We drove to another oil well.
> Manuel checked the water level, then he pointed west.
> "Over there, maybe seven miles, you'll find some adobe walls."
> He paused.
> "All that's left from a settlement of Spanish sheepherders."
>
> He nodded toward a mesa in the distance.
> "Some folks claim that Comanches held off the Calvary from up there."
>
> We climbed back in the truck.

This place, its history and its people, its dust, and its wind
are a part of us.

Vega, Texas.

It's not just your hometown.
It's a place that was assigned to you by God.

Graduates, tonight, as you look at the pictures of your life,
don't just look at your friends, look at the place.

This community. This town. This place called home.

FROM WILDERNESS TO GARDEN

Funeral

When I met with Brian's family
to prepare this funeral Mass,
we visited together for a long time.

> We needed to.
> We needed a long time
> to talk about such a good man.
> A man who is going to be missed
> more than words can begin to convey.

In our conversation,
I kept hearing words like:

> Athlete.
> Strong.
> Competitive.
> A man driven to do his best.
> A man who wanted everyone around to be the best person they could be.

These are qualities we admire in any person:

> They are indicative of a person who sets goals,
> maintains a clear focus
> and accomplishes many things.

> You might call these qualities "Outside Qualities"
> because they are readily apparent from the outside.

Yet, the longer I listened, the more I heard about a man whose
inner life was as deep and rich as his outer life.

> I heard about man who possessed a wonderful, cheerful laugh.
> A man who loved to work because he loved his family.
> A man who played golf with one son
> and worked at the same location as his other son
> Sons whom he coached in the way of true manhood...
> sons whom he supported and loved with all his strength.

> I also learned about a loving husband,

a soul-mate and devoted companion to his wife, Rita.
A man who reverenced God.
A solid man of strong character and integrity.

As I listened, I found myself thinking about the Book of Genesis
and how Brian's life
reflects the story of the first man, Adam.

Most people are not aware of this fact but,
if you read the Story of Creation closely,
you discover that, while Eve, the first woman, was created in the garden,
Adam was created in the wild.

God created Adam before He created the garden.
That is to say, the Rough Country,
> the Outback,
> the Frontier,
> the Desert.

> It would be an untamed place
> where Adam would have to prove his strength,
> demonstrate his ability to serve his God
> through providing for and protecting those around him.

> Eventually, of course, Adam found his true home inside the Garden.
> The Garden of Eden.

So it is that, within every man,
there remains that tension between
the Garden of Eden
and the Call of Adventure.

> One part of Adam longs to compete and achieve,
> another part of Adam savors a good meal
> surrounded by family.

One part of Adam hungers to be in control.
Another part of Adam longs to live in obedience to Truth
and in reverence of God.

I suspect that, for those of you who knew Brian well,
it was easy to see the influence of both sides of Adam.

This is how Brian lived.
This is also how he and Rita raised their family,

teaching their sons to be strong,
yet insisting that they be good.

Saint Augustine once wrote:
"You have made our hearts restless, O God,
and they remain restless until they rest in you."

When Augustine was a young man,
he experienced the tension between the two sides of Adam:
    the drive to be strong and resilient,
    and the need to be compassionate and merciful.

In the end,
this inherent tension in a man's life,
gives way to a sense of unity and peace.

It discovers this unity and peace
in the experience of mature, authentic and genuine love.

This is what St. Augustine meant when he said,
"Our lives are restless, until they rest in God."
Until they rest in God's love."

Throughout our life,
in our good times and our bad times,
in our achievements, our accomplishments
and even in our failures,
we continually reach for something just beyond our grasp,
yet this "something" is close enough to touch.

    It's like that vision of a new Jerusalem
    that we heard about in today's second reading from the Book of Revelation.

    That vision of God's love, as beautiful as a bride adorned for her husband.
    That place we long to be,
    yet remains up ahead, somewhere up the road.

    That place where all our work finally makes sense
    and all our striving comes to rest.
    That "new heaven, that new earth"
    where every tear is wiped away.

    Where there is no more death,
    no more separation,
    no more pain.
    Where the voice of the Savior rings loud and strong,

"Behold," he says. "Behold, I make all things new."

THE RIVERBANK

The Baptism of the Lord

Do you realize that certain places hold a kind of power over you?

Normally, we use the word *power* to describe people:
> The *fireman* who breaks down a door
> to rescue someone trapped inside a burning house
> is powerful.

We use *powerful to* describe certain words:
> The word *love* is a powerful word.

We even use it to describe certain experiences or events:
> That *play-off game?* Man, that was a powerful contest!

So, we describe people, words and events as powerful
but we don't often associate the word power with a particular place.

Today we celebrate the Baptism of the Lord.
We just heard the event described in the Gospel of St. Mark.
It was the beginning of Jesus' mission to redeem the world.
A *powerful* event!

> John the Baptist was a man filled with the *power* of God
> and he preached the word in a *powerful* way.

> On this particular day,
> the sky was ripped open!
> The voice of God boomed like thunder through the sky!

> How *powerful* of an experience must that have been?

But what about the place itself?
Did anyone of us, in hearing the story,
give a thought to the place where it unfolded?

> After all, what is there to see?
> A muddy river bank?

Sand? Rocks? Some tall grass?
Maybe the sound of rapids somewhere down stream?

Not much to say about the place.
The Bible itself provides no specific description of it.

Yet it does mention the place again.
And most of us are probably not aware of it.

It's only a passing reference,
but the Bible tells us that the place where Jesus was baptized
was, in fact, a place of power.

It held within it a distinct kind of *spiritual power*
and we learn about it toward the end of John's gospel.

Here's the setting:
Jesus' public ministry is coming to an end
and his career has taken a nosedive!

Most of his followers have abandoned him.
When he delivers the discourse on the Eucharist, they say,
"Who can endure this kind of talk?"
and the passage indicates that most of them abandon him.
He didn't deliver what they had hoped.
They were disillusioned and disgruntled.

On top of all this, the word on the street is that He is possessed
and the religious leaders are threatening him with arrest
and, at one point, someone in the crowd picks up a stone to hurl at him.

It was at this time that John's gospel mentions
that Jesus returns to the place of his baptism.
It states that he remains there for a significant period of time.

Why did he go back?
Was he hiding out like Billy the Kid or Bonnie and Clyde?

Hardly!

Rather, was he not drawn back to the place where his ministry began
in order to hear an echo of the words of his Father?

Words that would give him the courage to face the opposition and hatred.
Words that would give him the strength to endure
the torture and horrific death that would soon take place.

What were those words?
The words that rained down from heaven
the day the voice of God tore open the sky!
"You are my beloved Son; with you I am well pleased."

Fr. Jim Schmitmeyer

To get to those words...the Lord Jesus had to get to that place.

Seems odd, doesn't it?
How can a place have that kind of power?

These days, most us don't give much thought to the notion of place.
If we think of a place at all, it's just temporary,
some place we are just passing through, preferably at great speed.

With the onset of virtual reality, our notion of place is further diminished.

Some sociologists and theologians
note that this lack of appreciation for one's place
--one's roots, one's hometown, neighborhood or locality—
leads people to live lives that are inherently detached...
lives of endless choice and endless possibilities
which, in turn, means no loyalty and no commitment.

But our rootlessness and mobility and freedom from place
is an illusion.
A blind spot.

Places have meaning.
Places have power.

Consider this example:

There is a cathedral in Zanzibar.
The cathedral is large and inspiring
but its foundation is set deep in the soil
of a former marketplace where slaves once were sold.

> Those who designed and built the cathedral
> made certain that the high altar would be positioned
> precisely over the place
> where the whipping post once stood.

> That place of human degradation
> is of redemption, healing and hope.

Places are important.
And the places where we pray are especially important.

> We need these places
> like a child needs a mother
> like a husband needs his wife.

"You are my beloved Son; with you I am well pleased."

Jesus returned to the scene of his baptism
to recall the words of his Father's love.

Where do you go when you need that kind of place?
Where do you go to light a candle of hope?
Where do you go to catch a faint whisper of God voice saying:
　　"*You* are my son.
　　You are my daughter.
　　In you I am well pleased!" ?

Friends, never underestimate the power of a physical place
to put you in touch with a spiritual place.

That place deep in your heart
where you can hear the Word of God
strong, loud and clear:

YOU ARE **MINE. I LOVE YOU.**
IN YOU I AM WELL PLEASED!

THE FABRIC OF FAITH

Easter

On Easter morning,
    our songs,
    our prayers,
    our minds...
focus on the Empty Tomb.

    This is the glorious and victorious symbol of Easter:
    the Empty Tomb.

    But was it really empty?
    Completely empty?

No.
According to the Gospel of St. John,
there were two pieces of cloth left behind:
The burial cloth.
And the cloth that covered his head.

Ever notice how many cloths, garments and clothes
get mentioned in the life of Christ?
Let me list a few:

    the swaddling clothes
    in which his mother wrapped him
    on the night of his birth

    the hem of his garment brushed by the fingers
    of a woman suffering a chronic condition

    the towel that Jesus tied around his waist
    when he dried the feet of his disciples at the Last Supper

    the tunic ripped off a young man
    fleeing the Temple Guards on the night of Jesus' arrest

    the red cloak thrown across Jesus' shoulders,
    lacerated from the soldiers' whips

the veil that Veronica used to wipe his face on the way to Golgotha

the seamless garment on which the soldiers toss their dice

the curtain in the Temple ripped from top to bottom
at the moment that He died

the shroud in which He was buried.

These references to woven cloth are recorded in the Word of God for a reason.
They have been written down to help us believe:

Listen, once again, to the scene as described by John:

When Simon Peter arrived...he went into the tomb
and saw the burial cloths there,
and the cloth that had covered his head...
Then the other disciple also went in,
the one who had arrived at the tomb first,
and he saw...and believed.

How can a simple cloth help us to believe in something we can't see?

Years ago, a widow confided in me
a very poignant story from her life.

> She and her husband had been married more than fifty years.
> When her husband died,
> the woman grieved deeply.
> Her days were full of sorrow.
> And, at night, the only way she could fall asleep
> was to go to the closet in the bedroom,
> wrap herself in her husband's bath robe
> and go back to bed.

Ever think that a terrycloth bath robe
could serve as a channel of God's grace?

The story about the widow and the bathrobe brings to mind
how the power of love
was once woven into another robe,
the one mentioned in the story of the Prodigal Son.

We know the parable well: arrogant son tells his old man to drop dead

Fr. Jim Schmitmeyer

(I want my inheritance. Now!).

The old man hands over his hard-earned money
and the kid skips town...
lives wild, loses his job and, finally,
comes trudging home one day because he's hungry
and tired of feeding pigs.

But the boy's father never stopped hoping son would come home.
On the day he catches sight of him off in the distance, the father runs to him!

When he reaches his boy,
he tells the servants, to bring a robe for his back,
a ring for his finger
and shoes for his feet.

Why a ring for his finger?
So folks would look at the ring
and ignore the dirt and grease beneath the fingernails
and the fact that the hand is swollen and the knuckles are raw
from a fight in some parking lot behind some bar.

Then the father called for a pair of shoes
because his son had become a barefoot bum.

And now the robe. Why the robe?
If you ask me, it was because the kid was shirtless
and dirty
and stunk like a pig
and so skinny you count his ribs.

An amazing story. Instead of dressing down the kid,
the father dresses him up!

Can something as simple as a garment on your back
help you to believe in a God you can't see?

In the Book of the Prophet Isaiah we read,
"I rejoice greatly in the LORD,
for He has clothed me with the garment of salvation,
He has wrapped me with a robe of righteousness!"

How has the Lord clothed you?

Has it ever occurred to you that
Christ left those burial clothes behind

because he didn't need them?
His Body—resurrected—shines with divine glory.
What need has He of earthly clothes?

Has it ever occurred to you
that He left behind those hand-me-downs
for *you*?

> Like a bathrobe to warm a soul that is cold
> and frigid
> and shivering from grief?

> Like a football jersey on the back of an athlete
> who runs out on the field
> pumping his legs and his arms beneath the Friday night lights,
> determined to play his best
> and make his parents proud all over again?

How has the Lord clothed you?

> When you turned fifteen,
> did He clothed you with love
> as beautiful and bright
> as a quinceañera dress?

> After you graduated from school,
> did He clothe you with the quiet dignity
> of a work uniform?
> A military uniform?
> A nurse's uniform?
> A fire-fighter's uniform?

How has the Lord clothed you?

> When you gouged yourself with the sharp knife of sin,
> did he arrive with bandages and swab your wounds?

> When the insults of Satan stripped you naked,
> did Christ appear and hand you a towel
> to cover your shame
> until you could get to Confession
> where He would clothe you
> with the cloak of the prodigal son?

Friends, on this holy feast of Easter,
keep in mind that Christ did not leave the Empty Tomb

49

completely empty.

Rather, He left behind some holy garments.

He left behind those funeral garments
and clothed himself in a robe of Life...a glorified Life,
    the Life of his Divine and Holy Spirit,
    the Spirit of God
    who fills the Church with the Light of Truth
    and fills each soul with the Light of Faith.

What a glorious day, this holy feast of Easter!
When believers throughout the world
stand at the mouth of an open tomb,
gaping at clothes left behind...
and gazing...
    gazing with unbridled joy
    at the Glory that lies ahead.

A MASTERPIECE!

Quinceañera

All men and women are entrusted with the task of crafting their own life;
they are, in a certain sense, to make of it a work of art, a masterpiece.
—St. Pope John Paul II

When you ask a high school student,
    "What do you like to do? What are you good at?"

    Nine times out of ten, they will say,
    "I'm good at math. Or, I play in the band.
    Or, I enjoy sports. I run track. I play volleyball."

    When I asked Carmen what she like to do,
    without hesitation, she said:
    "I'm an artist. I like to draw."

That statement illustrates the beautiful vision of St. John Paul II:
"All men and women are entrusted with the task
of making their life a work of art, a masterpiece."

The Book of Genesis reminds us that, as children of God,
we are part of his masterpiece, the greatest work of art ever created.

In the Book of Psalms, we read,
"When I look at the heaven which you have made,
the moon and stars which you have set in place,
who are we that you have made us little less than the angels?"

    The person who wrote that psalm, had to have been an artist.
    A true artist cannot look at the world
    without recognizing the magnificent handiwork of God.

    An artist is a person who looks at the world
    and beholds its vibrant colors,
    the movement of the leaves on the trees,
    the texture of waves on the water,
    the dance of sunlight in the eyes of a child.

    The artist sees the shadows and shapes of mountains

Fr. Jim Schmitmeyer

and the soft petals of roses...
and longs to hold these beautiful things close to her heart
the way a child holds a tiny bird in her hand.

The artist is the person who teaches the rest of us
the meaning of reverence.

A famous theologian once said,
"A person who no longer recognizes beauty
will soon forget how to pray."

Today, Carmen takes an important step in her life as a child of God.
She renews her baptismal promises
and dedicates herself to Mary, the Mother of our Lord.

She has already begun to do this!

In developing her skills and talents as an artist,
Carmen had shown us
that, like Mary, she longs to hold life, with all its beauty
close to her heart.

And Mother Mary, who shows us the deepest reverence of all,
will surely guide Carmen in the deep longing of her soul
to capture the beauty of God's world in her works of art.

But this is not the only way in which Mary has inspired this young person
to draw close to God.

Through the deep love of her parents,
through their example and teaching,
through their dedication to the Catholic faith,
their love of the holy sacraments and the lives of the saints,
Mary has already been guiding Carmen
to not only appreciate the beauty of the world around her,
but she has led Carmen to a profound respect for the gift of life itself.

Yes, Carmen has the eye of an artist,
but she also has the heart of a mother.

When I asked Carmen about her vocation
and where she hears God calling her,
she immediately answered that she wants to be a doctor
who helps women bring new life into the world.

What a wonderful vision, what an amazing dream
God has planted in her heart!

Carmen, each one of us here today:
your parents who love you so much,

52

your brother and sister who admire you so deeply,
your friends who appreciate your kind gentleness so truly,
we are, all of us, filled with joy and we give thanks to God
for the good work that He has begun in you.

May you continue to obey his commandments
and follow the Lord with all your heart.

> May your life, indeed, be a work of art,
> a masterpiece of divine beauty.

AN OUTDOOR GOD

Baptism

"Here in Texas," a farmer once told me,
"everything either sticks you, pricks you or bites you."

He wasn't bragging, just stating facts.

No doubt,
this was a guy who had
strung barbed wire,
shot rattlers
and gathered cattle in pastures choked with mesquite.

It was clear that he felt a certain pride from living in a place where everything
sticks you, pricks you or bites you."

In today's gospel, we hear about Jesus heading out to the desert.

For me, it's not hard to imagine him like some Texas farmer,
a guy with a face set like flint,
an axe in one hand,
a shotgun in the other.
A man well-acquainted with thorns, snakes and scorpions.

Today, at this Mass, we baptize Greg and Rebecca's third son, Jacob.Somehow, it
seems appropriate that we do so on this first Sunday of Lent that tells us about
an outdoor Savior.
A Savior whose mettle is tested in the desert.
A Savior whose strength blazes like the sun,
whose power and authority presses down into the soul
like the heat of a West Texas summer day.

Greg and Rebecca earn their livelihood from their farm.
So this boy of theirs is going to grow up on the land.

He'll learn, early on,
that God will speak to him
  not only in the Words of the Bible
  not only in the Sacraments of the Church;
  not only through his upbringing in a Catholic home...

but the Lord will also speak to him in the wind
that will someday chaff his face
through the sun that will bronze his skin
through the open plains that will draw his eyes to the horizon.

Today, at this baptism,
we are reminded that our God, our creator,
is first and foremost,
an outdoor God.

Today, His power and strength,
enters into the soul of this child
like the wind that once hovered over the primordial waters;

Today, each one of us gathered here in this country church,
will witness His compassion and mercy, like the sun,
renewing our community,
giving it growth in numbers and in faith.

And we, ourselves, give thanks for our salvation in Christ,
who overcame the trials of the desert
and the power of death to bring us the promise of life,
eternal life in Him.

NEW GAME, NEW RULES

Thanksgiving Day

In Bible times, leprosy was a common affliction.
The Book of Leviticus devotes two whole chapters to the disease:
it instructs priests how to diagnose the disease;
it the instructs lepers on how far they had to live outside of town...
    in caves...like animals.

The Book of Leviticus also instructed lepers
in proper attire, personal grooming and social etiquette:

> Their clothes had to be torn.
> Their hair had to hang loose.
> If they were to meet anyone on the road,
> they had to shout, "Unclean, unclean!"

Those were the rules.
The ten lepers in today's gospel followed those rules.

So, when the lepers began to shout and holler,
Jesus and his disciples obviously looked their way.

> What did they see?
> They saw people with faces hollow from hunger,
> bodies scarred by the flesh-eating disease.

What happens next?

Jesus yells back to them,
"Go show yourselves to the priests."

And off they go!
They knew the rules.

> They knew that, according to the rules in the Book of Leviticus,
> only a priest could declare a leper clean and free.

> Until then,
> they were to draw near to no one else
> except another leper.

> So they followed the rules.

> Why wouldn't they?
> For years, they had lived like wounded coyotes,

far from town,
with torn skin and matted hair.

They had no choice.
Those were the rules.
And they followed the rules.
All except one.

One of them broke rank.
One of them broke the rules.
One of them did *not* do as he was told.

Overcome with the healing of Christ...
a healing that was now flowing through him
like the surge of blood into a limb that was numb,
the Samaritan leper broke the rules,
turned around and ran back to Jesus!

The passage says that he fell at his feet... and thanked him!

Can you see it?
Tears of joy mingled with the dust on the road.
Can you imagine the scene?

His friends headed to Jerusalem to get their health certificates.
but this man was on his knees giving his life to Christ.

Nine lepers followed the rules.
the tenth leper followed his heart.

Today is Thanksgiving Day.
Most of us, I suspect,
think of *thanksgiving* as something we do:

We thank God for our blessings.
And then we move on.

That's what Thanksgiving Day entails:
We say a prayer of thanks for the food,
then get on with the meal,
followed by a football game.
It's an important day... and it has its own set of rules.

But true gratitude doesn't follow those kinds of rules.
Gratitude isn't about following rules.
As much as it is about falling in love.

Thanksgiving is good as far as it goes.
But gratitude takes us farther, much farther.

In terms of today's gospel:

57

Fr. Jim Schmitmeyer

Following the rules gets you a certificate,
but gratitude leads you to God.

Gratitude, as one wise person once put it,
is the essence of sainthood.

We are called to be saints.
We are called to give thanks.

[Note: The author is indebted to Rev. Barbara Brown Taylor whose Thanksgiving Day homily in *The Preaching Life* provided key insights and much of the content of this homily.]

A GRAIN OF WHEAT

The Feast of St. Isidore the Farmer

Do you ever get homesick?

> Are there are times when your mind goes back to the little yard
> where your grandmother fed chickens?
>
> Or a ranch where your family and neighbors
> gathered cattle and branded calves?
>
> When away on vacation, do you yearn to return home?
>
> If you ever get homesick like that,
> you are very fortunate.
> You are fortunate because you know what it means
> to love the place where you live.

Last November, the large health care provider, *Cigna*,
conducted a nationwide survey.
The survey found that most Americans suffer
from strong feelings of loneliness.

> At first glance, this seems like a superficial problem.
> But, according to *Cigna*, it is a serious condition.
> More serious than it sounds.
> Especially when you realize that, in many ways, loneliness is killing us.
>
> The suicide rate and drug overdoses are skyrocketing.
> This year, in our country, 45,000 people
> will take their own lives.
> Nearly 70,000 people will die from a drug overdose
> (this last figure is greater than the number of all the soldiers who died
> in the ten-year Viet Nam War).

Yes, loneliness is killing us.

Why are we becoming so lonely?

Fr. Jim Schmitmeyer

One reason, I believe, is that people have forgotten the importance
of loving the place where they live.

In a world where people hop from job to job,
and from city to city,
deep roots are hard to come by.

But this is where people like us
have an important mission to fulfill.
People like us.
People who live in rural America.

We are being called to show the rest of the country
of how important it is
to love the place where you live.

My dad was a farmer.
He never made it past the 3rd grade.
But he taught his children everything they needed to know.

He taught us to say our prayers
and he taught the difference between right and wrong.

And he also taught us this:
"To be close to the soil, is to be close to God."

What does it mean to be "close to the soil?"

It means to be like a grain of wheat
that falls to the soil,
then gives its life
so that others might live.

To give one's life
requires deep love,
love for the people and the place where you live.

Last month, the columnist for the New York Times, David Brooks,
wrote an article entitled, "What Rural America Has to Teach Us."
Here is a brief excerpt:

Everybody says rural America is collapsing.
But that's not what I see.

For example, I spent this past week in Nebraska.
The towns are not rich.
At many of the schools, 50 percent of the students receive free or reduced-cost lunch.
But the crime is low. Many people leave their homes and cars unlocked.

One woman I met came home and noticed her bedroom light was on.
She thought it was her husband home early.
But it was her plumber.
She'd mentioned at the coffee shop that she had a clogged sink,
so he'd swung round, let himself in and fixed it.

When she needs some auto work done,
she leaves a blank check on the front seat of the car.
The town mechanic comes by when he can,
drives the car to his garage, does the work and fills out the check.

What Mr. Brooks ends up saying is that
too many Americans don't have a place they think of as home.

A place with a "hometown gym feeling" on a Friday night.

It is no secret to anyone
that we have a lot of problems and division in our country.

With God's help, rural Americans can help heal that division.

When you love where you live,
most differences — economic differences, political differences — seem trivial.

In a country suffering from loneliness,
each of us can help America start to heal
when we start to put our communities, our schools and our churches first.

In short, when we become the kind neighbors
and generous friends
that the Lord calls us to be.

> "Unless a grain of wheat falls to the earth and dies,
> it remains a grain of wheat.
> But, if it dies,
> it produces a hundredfold."

MOON BLOSSOMS

Funeral

Most of us,
when we think about time,
think of ourselves as moving forward...
moving forward through time
and toward the future.

In thinking this way, unfortunately,
we turn our back on the past.

On a day like this, however,
it is fitting and appropriate to spend some time
thinking about the past.

> As today's reading from Ecclesiastes puts it:
> *For everything there is a season,*
> *And a time for every matter under heaven.*

Sometimes—oftentimes—our daily schedules,
packed tight with things to get done and places to go,
do not unfold the way we expect.

I was reminded of that a few days ago
while sitting on the porch
of Lizet and Carlos's house.

> If you've been to their house,
> you know that there are huge bushes
> with gigantic blossoms
> in front of that porch.

> It was late afternoon.
> The blossoms on these plants
> were just beginning to open.

> Carlos explained to me that these beautiful flowers,
> white and pink,
> bloom only at night.
> They are called Four O'clocks

because that's the time their blossoms tend to open:
four o'clock in the afternoon.

They bloom at night, when few people notice.

Those blossoms reminded me of Lizet.
Her life, as delicate and beautiful as a blossom,
bloomed inside her house...
where few people noticed.

After a vigorous life of serving her community
in the fields of mental health and criminal justice,
Lizet, at the age of 40, was diagnosed with MS.

> For the next twenty-four years,
> she would live her life at home, inside her house,
> confined to a bed.

> A flower blooming in a place where few people notice.

But for those
who knew her
and loved her
and cared for her,
> we know that flowers that bloom in the dark
> are among the most cherished flowers of all.

> Ask Carlos
> who bought those Four O'clocks and planted them
> the day he and Lizet moved into that house.

> Ask their daughter, Kendi,
> who stayed with her and assisted in her care
> hour after hour, day after day.

> Flowers that bloom in the dark,
> when the rest of the world fails to notice,
> are among the most cherished of all.

For everything there is a season,
And a time for every matter under heaven.

Yes, some flowers bloom in the dark.

Fr. Jim Schmitmeyer

But God's idea of time is not the same as ours and his flowers bloom
anytime, anywhere he desires them to bloom.

God's time is not our time.

In our world, time always runs out.
In God's world, time never ends.

The New Testament was written in Greek
and the Greek language has two different words for Time:
Chronos and Kairos.

Chonos refers to the kind of time that we can measure.
Kairos refers to those moments in life when time seems to stand still.

> The Book of Revelation describes this special kind of time
> as beyond anything we can imagine,
> telling us that, on that day that will never end,
> the skies will open
> and there will be a New Earth and a New Heaven
> where there will be no more death or crying out or pain...
> when every tear is wiped away.

We have the assurance of this from Jesus himself.

Do not let your hearts be troubled, he said.
There are many rooms in my Father's House.

Like those apostles,
Lizet placed her faith in Christ
and in the promises of Christ.

Among those promises is the assurance that he has prepared a place for us
in the House of the Father.

In that special place,
Lizet won't find any clocks.
Nor will she find any Four O'clock flowers.

> Because, in heaven, time is eternal.
> If there be flowers, they bloom all day, all night!
>
> Like flowers that never fade,
> we pray that the love of God

will enfold her forever.

THE WORK OF OUR HANDS

Labor Day

Today is Labor Day.

When it comes to different jobs and professions,
the Bible contains a broad selection:
For instance, we find
> fishermen,
> carpenters
> and farmers.

> Mary was a stay-at-home mom,
> Lydia traded in fabric,
> Tabitha was a seamstress.

> We find many professions represented:
> > tax collectors,
> > table waiters,
> > sailors,
> > soldiers,
> > rabbis and teachers,
> > kings and astronomers.

Naturally, when a Bible passage mentions your own line of work,
you sit up and listen.

The Parable of the Sower gets a farmer thinking about fertilizer and herbicide.
The story of Jairus, the Roman centurion, gets a nod from a member of the National Guard.

Look hard enough, you can find a biblical counter-part
to almost every kind of modern-day profession or trade.

So, what profession comes to mind when we listen to today's second reading about the human body?

"Offer your body as a pleasing sacrifice to the Lord," writes St. Paul.

Doctors and nurses hear this passage and start thinking:
> heart rate,

blood pressure,
body temperature.

Chiropractors and physical therapists are suddenly considering
muscle tone and joint alignment.

So, why does St. Paul draw our attention to the human body
when speaking about offering a worthy sacrifice to the Lord?

Well, his starting point has nothing to do
with sprained ankles
or ruptured disks
or ruptured spleens.

Rather, in Pauline theology,
there exists a vital, intricate connection
between physical realities and spiritual realities.

One is the mirror of the other.

For instance:
the weight of guilt
makes your soul
stooped and slouched.

The sin of arrogance
gives you a stiff neck.

And too much self-reliance
atrophies the muscle called
Faith-in-God.

Keep in mind that, if you happen to hire
Paul the apostle as your personal trainer,
his attention will include more than just your own muscle tone,
his main concern is the health and condition of the Church itself,
in particular, our own parish.

And this is where St. Paul's alignment of body and soul
proves its genius.

Because, you see, in the outside world,
people get trampled on a regular basis.
It's a dog-eat-dog jungle, as they say,
and the world is built on competition.

But it's not that way in the church.
In the body of the Church, like the body of a human being,
harmony and healing go hand-in-hand.

"A foot can't say, 'Because I am not a hand I do not belong to the body,'
An ear can't say, 'Because I am not an eye I do not belong to the body!'"

This means that, in our own parish, as in every other parish,
when you cut someone down,
it's kind of like cutting off your hand!

"The foot cannot live without a hand," says St. Paul.
"We are all part of one another."

Yes, as a Catholic parish, we are one body: the Body of Christ.
And when we wound one another...we slap Christ in the face.

Thanks be to God, I seldom observe this taking place.
But I know that I occasionally need this reminder.
I suspect other folks need it, as well.

Pope Francis once said,
"How I long for the church to become
an island of mercy
in an ocean of despair."

What does this mean?
He means that,
in the Church,
we must strive to excel at mercy, not competition.

Despite the sins we commit
and the wounds that we inflict,
Christ desires that we be healed.

And the most effective healing
comes from hands like His...
that is, hands that are *pierced*.

> Think of how this plays out in our day-to-day:
> the most effective healing flows
> from those who, themselves, have been wounded.
>
> We call this forgiveness.
> We call it mercy.
> As when a father forgives his teenage son
> who wrecked the car
> and they shake hands;
>
> As when hands that you once shoved away

return to lift you up
when sickness strikes
or your own arrogance
causes you to stumble and fall.

Whether we are speaking of spiritual realities, such as forgiveness,
or physical realities, such as mutual aid and assistance,
we live within an intricate matrix of hands.

I recall the words of a sociologist
that related this reality in a poignant way.
The words went something like this:
> *We live within an immense movement of hands.*
> *The hands of other people lift us from the womb.*
> *The hands of other people who grow the food we eat,*
> *weave the clothes that we wear*
> *and build the structures that we inhabit.*
> *The hands of other people provide solace in moments of tenderness*
> *and comfort in times of distress.*
> *And, in the end, the hands of other people*
> *will lower us into the grave.*

On this Labor Day,
we give thanks to God for all the ways that the hands of other people
serve the human community.

And here, within the community of the Church,
we give thanks
for all the corporal works of mercy that we give and receive:
> that is to say,
> the offering of the work of our hands
> for the glory of Christ Jesus
> and the building up of the God's Kingdom in this world.

HEROD, THE PITIFUL

The Epiphany

Why go to the movies when you can go to Mass instead?

Why settle of *The Game of Thrones* when the Feast of the Epiphany
offers the same kind of drama?

> Nighttime visions!
> Ancient Prophecies!
> A Secret Code!
> A threatened baby!
> And a nasty villain named Herod!

Herod.

Did you know that he not only killed the baby boys of Bethlehem,
history also records that he killed his own sons
for fear of losing his throne?

Herod. A figure that inspires disgust.

Is there anything more pitiful
than a powerful man
who is afraid of a vulnerable child?

Why do the Herods of the world fear children?

> I believe it because the face of a child
> brings the powerful of the world
> face to face with the power of love
> in a way that nothing else can.

Our faith teaches us that
there is no power on earth
greater than the power of love.

The powerful Herod was afraid of a powerless infant!

Yet, the force of love is stronger than the power of fear.

Is this the reason God himself entered our broken world
as an infant child
of a refugee couple?

My friends, no Hollywood adventure film can compare
to the high drama of the Epiphany.

Indeed, the story of Christmas is not complete
until we take our place in the scene where the Magi offer their homage,
not to the high and mighty Herod,
but to the lowly child of the Virgin Mary,
the Son of the Most High God!

In this ancient story, the salvation of the world hangs in balance.
God reveals to the Magi the secret to peace:
> the secret that there will be peace in the world
> when every leader, every government,
> every man and every woman
>
> honor not only the holy child held in Mary's arms
> but every child
> held in the arms of every mother
> everywhere and every place in the world.

71

SIGNS ALONG THE WAY

Wedding

Can you imagine getting behind the wheel of your car or truck,
setting off down the road
and suddenly discovering
that there are no road signs along the way?
Nor any other signs of any kind?

> No highway numbers...to let you know if you happen to be on I-40 or I-27.
> No state lines.
> No county lines.
> No city limit signs.

> Imagine a road trip with no exit signs.
> No speed limit signs,
> No hotel signs,
> No restaurant signs,
> No street signs,
> No warning signs,
> No names on the water towers of the small towns you drive through.

Do you ever think about this?
> How much we rely on signs
> each time we get behind the wheel of a vehicle?

It'd feel as though you were in a Science Fiction movie.
It'd be unnerving and disorienting, to say the least.

After all, we need signs to tell us
where we are
and point us to
where we hope to go.

We can't imagine a world without signs.

Maybe that's one reason why St. John the Evangelist,
the patron saint of this parish church,
used the word, "sign," instead of miracle, when he wrote his gospel.

The other three gospels, Matthew, Mark and Luke

spend a lot of time focusing on Jesus' miracles:
>the healing of a leper
>restoring sight to the blind
>raising a dead person from life.

But when St. John talks about these events, calls them *signs*.

And the first miraculous sign in the Gospel of St. John
is the one you and I just heard:
the story, the miracle, that Lisa and Jose
chose to be read to their wedding Mass:

>the amazing event that occurred at a wedding reception
>where the wine ran out
>and Jesus turned 180 gallons of water
>into vintage wine so the party could continue
>without interruption.

"Jesus performed the first of his signs,"
says the gospel,
"at a wedding in Cana."

Yes, this was miracle.
An amazing miracle.
But it was also a *sign*.

>This word puts us back behind the wheel of a car
>driving down the Interstate, does it not?

>This word reminds us that,
>just as we need signs posted along the road
>to get us to Santa Fe or Denver,
>so, too, we rely on signs from heaven
>to help us navigate the journey of our life.

One of the things I most enjoy about helping a young couple
like Jose and Lisa prepare for the Sacrament of Marriage,
is finding out how good they are at reading signs.

How good are they are recognizing the signs of God's love in their lives?

I have to say that this young couple passed "the driving test" with ease!

The first sign of God's love that they encountered was firmly planted
within their own families.

They spoke of the good example they received from their parents:

> Faith in God
> Compassion for one another
> Caring for one another, sacrificing for one another

> They went on to talk about all the other signs
> of community that they witness and experience here in their parish,
> from catechism classes to babysitting to spaghetti dinners...
> the more they gave, the more they received.

As far as what lies ahead up the road, they are excited about how, someday, they will share the story of their faith with their children.

They know the signs and can read them well.

For us Catholics, the most necessary signs of all are called Sacraments.

What do we mean by the word *sacrament?*

Well, a sacrament *is* a sign, but not just an ordinary sign.

Obviously, a sacrament is a sign that points to God.
> But that's just the beginning.
> A sacrament not only points to God.
> A sacrament not only takes you to God.
> A sacrament actually makes you a part of God!!

On the day that Jesus changed water into wine
at a wedding in Cana,
he not only made the wine a sign of the power his love,
he made the young couple a sign of his own love as well.

For the rest of their lives,
that married couple at Cana would be known as the couple at whose wedding
Jesus, the Son of God, first revealed his presence in the world.

A type of sacrament, so to speak,
reminding them and their hometown,
that God's love never runs empty,
rather, it floods our life like rich, red wine at a wedding reception.

Lisa and Jose,
today, by the power of the Holy Spirit,
your love is transformed into a Sacrament!

With the two of you in our lives,
living out your love for each other with all your strength and all your hearts,
we—your families, your parish, your community—we are given a sign,
a wonderful sign, that points us to God Himself...
a sign that points us to God who lives in our midst.

A sign that tells us that Christ,
the Son of God and the Savior of the world
is traveling this road alongside us,
filling every empty jar to the brim, changing the water
of our weakness and fears into wine,
the rich wine, of grace and redemption.

You have passed the driver's test.
Pay attention to the signs along the way
so as to arrive, one day,
safe and secure,
at our Father's House.

THE MAN FROM GESARA

Funeral

On days like this, people will say they came "to say good-bye."

But how can we bring ourselves to say good-bye to a young man,
strong and athletic, vibrant and courageous,
a man like Josh,
when every fiber in our being yells out,
"Stay! Stay with us! We can't live without you!"

Is this not true?
Is this not what each one of us feels at this moment?

How can we bid farewell to a likeable young guy
with a winning smile, always ready with a warm embrace?

> A hard worker, a natural leader,
> a loving uncle tossing his nephew into the air,
> a brother, a cousin teaching you to play ball,
> a son, helpful and protective,
> a friend, sensitive and supportive...

how can we say good-bye to someone like Josh?

It is not possible.
So, what do most Christians do at time like this?

> We turn to the Word of God,
> the promises of Christ
> and the power of the Holy Spirit:

> *Though I walk in the Valley of the Shadow of Death*
> *I fear no evil...*
> *for you, Lord, are there...*
> *with your rod and your staff that guide me.*

Now, *I* believe the Word of God. And *you* believe the Word of God.
But how can this Word of God *get through* to us today?

How can its promise of Light and Life
penetrate our minds and take hold of our hearts
as you and I trudge through the long shadows of this dark valley?

Where is our hope in this dark hour?
What strength can we muster?

Let's start by focusing, not on the Word of God,
but on some words from Josh.

I'm thinking here of something Josh once said to his grandmother.
Here is the story:

> Josh had just walked into the kitchen
> and the skin on his arm was all scuffed up
> from some football game or practice.

She asked him,
"Why do you this to yourself, Josh?
Why must you play so hard?"

"Grandma," he said, "You can't hold back.
You have to give it your all."

You have to give it your all.

Sounds a lot like St. Paul:
"Run to win!!

"Be like the runners in a marathon,"
writes the great apostle.
"Run to win!"

In other words, *give it your all*!

Now, let me ask you young people,

> What do you most admire in an athlete?
> What quality separates a true athlete from a half-hearted athlete?

> A lot of good words could supply a good answer:
> Commitment
> Discipline
> Perseverance
> Let me add one more:
> Resilience, as in resilience in the face of pain.

> Great athletes demonstrate resilience
> when they "play through the pain."
> In any sport, in any worthwhile endeavor,
> there are times when it is necessary
> "to play through the pain."

I look around this church today and,
if you ask me, that's exactly what you and I are doing right now:
We are playing through the pain.

> Like the spiritual athletes St. Paul challenges us to be.

On a tough day like this,

our hearts pound,

our muscles ache...

but, together, we push forward,
we strain ahead...
we reach for the goal
and grab hold of our faith...

our faith in the power of Christ to save us.

There is a story in the Bible
about a man who was deeply troubled.

He lived among the tombs,
on the edge of town,
in the darkness of a cave
and no one dared to draw close.

Despite the best efforts of his family and community,
this man had separated himself from the rest of the world.

He would accept no help.
He refused any offer of friendship or love.

Yet, when Jesus visited the town called Gesara,
he sought out that man
whose soul, like the soul of a young man named Josh,
was filled with darkness and pain.

Without a moment of hesitation,
the Lord, upon learning of the man and his condition,
left the town of Gesarea
and went to the tombs

And there, alone with that troubled man,
he healed his pain
and restored him to life.

Do not overlook what preceded the healing:
The Lord *went into the tombs.*
The Lord entered into the darkness.
The Lord brought light to a place
that no one was able to do so.

There is no darkness so deep
that the light of God can't reach.

Will he not do the same for Josh?
Will he not do the same for us?

> *The Lord is my Shepherd, I shall not want.*
> *Though I walk in the valley of the shadow of death*
> *I fear no evil.*
> *For you are with.*
> *You have prepared a banquet for me.*
> *And I shall dwell in the House of the Lord*
> *All my days.*

Eternal rest grant unto Josh, oh Lord.
And let perpetual light shine upon him.

THINGS OF HEAVEN

The Ascension of the Lord

Here is a quick snapshot of American Values:
(as reported in the Los Angeles Times)

There are 300,000 items in average American homes.
Twenty-five percent of people with two-car garages
do not have room inside those garages to park even one car.
The average 10-year-old owns 238 toys!

For some of us, it's hard to let go of things we possess.
Yet, today's Feast of the Ascension of the Lord into Heaven
is about "letting go."

> Today's feast is about "not clinging to something we can touch."

> Today's feast is about surrendering that which gives us a sense of security.

As Americans, we aren't comfortable with letting things slip beyond our grasp:

The Lord ascends to heaven...out of our reach.
The Lord ascends to heaven...suddenly we are on our own.
The Lord ascends to heaven...and we are left alone and insecure.

Does it surprise you that this is the way the Gospel story ends?
It shouldn't surprise you at all.

> What did the Lord say to Mary Magdalene at the tomb on the day of Easter?
> *Do not cling to me...I have not yet ascended to my Father.*

> What did the Lord say to his disciples
> the day he called them to follow him?
> *Sell what you have, give to the poor, then come follow me.*

> What did the Lord instruct his followers to carry with them
> when he sent them out on mission?
> *On your journey through the villages, take with you no money,*
> *no sandals, no extra tunic.*

The gospel story is very consistent on this matter.
The things of earth do not matter...the things of Heaven do.

FIELDS OF GRACE

Wedding

There is a saying in the Bible that goes like this:

"A man will choose the direction in which to go,
but the Lord will guide his steps."

There's a lot of wisdom in that verse.

It reminds us that…
your plans, your hopes, your dreams…
the plans you have for our life…
are only your plans *in part*.

Because, always at work
    beneath our plans…
    and within our plans…
    is the deeper plan of God.

Consider a young woman.
She has a dream for her life.
She dreams of reaching out to the world
and holding it like a flower in her hand…

She longs to give from the deepest part of her heart.

She longs to live her life with honor and beauty,
dignity and purpose…

This is her plan.
But it is not only her plan.

Her plan is also a part of God's plan.

It is God's plan
that through her life,
His plans for the world will continue to unfold.

    A world of love, healing and peace—unfolding like a flower

for all his people.

In a similar way, a young man, in the words of the Bible,
leaves his father and mother and clings to his wife.

In doing this, he sets out from home with a plan.
A plan to be a hard worker,
to be a man of honesty and integrity,
to be a man who is strong, loving and wise.

In short, to be the best husband
and the best father he can be.

What an adventure…
to have a plan like this!

There is a name for this adventure.
We call it the Sacrament of Marriage.

A plan in which, day after day,
we chose our direction
yet allow God to guide our steps.

How do we know when our plans
coincide with God's plans?

Well, if the word *sacrament* describes the adventure,
the word *grace* sets it in motion.

What is grace?

Grace is what shows up in the journey of life
to let you know that you're on the right road.

Let me give you some examples:
Grace is what happens
at the end of a hard day
on a farm in West Texas
and a husband and a wife
kneel at the side of their bed in prayer.

Even though the weather has turned dry,

and the leaves on their crops
have curled into sharp spikes.
the man and woman offer the work of that day to God.

And in the cadence of their voices,
in the rise and fall of their prayers,
they sense the steadiness of God...
in the reality of their faith.

This is grace.

Here's another example:
On a summer morning,
light slants through a bedroom window,
and a man places his hand on the soft skin of his wife...
and feels the movement of new life within her.

This is grace.

Or again:
Neighbors are in need.
Their fences are down.
Their cattle get out.
The well runs dry.
A tractor breaks down.

Whatever the emergency might be,
the man and woman know what they must do...and they do it.

They drop their plans for the day, the week, the month...
as long as necessary until their neighbor is back on his feet.
This is grace.

Jesus once proposed this option:
"You can build a house on rock.
Or you can build a house on sand."

Those of us who know Jana and Steve
know what sort of foundation
on which they set marriage.

And we have not doubt that
their plan for their life is God's plan as well.

WELCOME HOME!

Funeral

What comes to mind when you hear the word *house?*
Naturally, you picture in your mind some sort of house.
You might picture a bungalow on a suburban street.
Or a farmhouse on a country road.
A young boy might picture a tree house
in the branches of a backyard maple.
A young girl might imagine a dollhouse
on the floor of the bedroom
that she shares with her big sister.

In our minds, the word *house* can conger up
lots of images
of different *kinds* of houses.

But what about the word *home?*
What comes to mind when you hear the word *home?*

> No doubt, when you hear the word *home,*
> the mental image is not going to be
> just any ol' house along some street in Celina or St. Mary's;
> it won't be just any ol' house along U.S. Route127.

> No.
> Rather, the word *home* will bring to mind
> a very particular place
> with very particular feelings
> and that particular place is the place you call home.

> The word *house* and the word *home* are connected.
> But their meanings are very different.

> So, with that in mind, listen again to these words
> from the Gospel of St. John:

Do not let your hearts be troubled, says the Lord.
In my Father's House, there are many dwelling places.
(Some translations say, many mansions:
In my Father's House, there are many mansions.)

Regardless of the word employed by translators,
we all know what the Lord means.

> He is not speaking about a *house*.
> He is not speaking about a physical structure or a shelter.
> He talking about a *home*.

> *I have gone to prepare a place for you,* says the Lord.
> *So that where I am, you also may be.*

> A more accurate translation of this verse would sound something like this:

> *In my Father's House,* says the Lord,
> *you will find your* home, *your true and eternal* home.

In the course of her life, my sister, Alberta, lived in many different houses.

> The farmhouse on our homeplace at Ft. Loramie.
> The house in the woods at Osgood
> where she and Leroy lived as newly weds.
> Then back to Ft. Loramie,
> to the house of our grandmother
> when our grandmother needed
> someone to take care of her.

I think of Alberta in each one of these places.
I picture her in the living rooms, the back yards, the front porches.

> Each house was different,
> but the atmosphere inside each house was always the same:
> it was that wonderful feeling you always felt
> in Alberta's presence...
> a happy, unassuming love
> conveyed in the warmth of her smile
> and the sparkle in her eyes.

Do not let your hearts be troubled, says the Lord.
I have prepared a place for you, a wonderful place.

When our grandmother died,

Fr. Jim Schmitmeyer

Leroy and Alberta and their young family moved here to Coldwater.

How many of you remember the house on East Main?
I do.
I remember the meals we ate in the small kitchen.
I recall the assistance
that Alberta extended to Mrs. Rowl, her next door neighbor.
And the help she offered to her mother-in-law, Polly,
in the house just the across the back yard.

Like the house at Ft. Loramie,
that house on East Main was Alberta's "base of operations"
from which she carried out all of her corporeal works of mercy.
Later on, there was the house on North Second Street,
across from the school,
the house that her boys called home in their teenage years,
(as did some students from Germany and the Netherlands);

a simple house wherein lived a mother
who wanted nothing more
than to survive the scourge of cancer
that had invaded her body,
so as to raise her boys
with the kind of love
that only a mother can provide.

The next house that Alberta and Leroy lived in
was near the community park.

There, as you would expect,
cheerfulness greeted you at the door,
joy danced as bright as the light in the windows
and compassion flowed from inside its rooms

out to the street...and on south to Versailles
where her own mother now suffered with Alzheimer's.
Alberta's help was needed and, as always, she responded,
responded with all she had to give,

even as she herself, at this time,
began a long and difficult struggle
with additional issues related to her health,
issues that brought with them
a lot of darkness and confusion.

Lord, we don't know where you are going, said Phillip.
How can we know the way?
How can we possibly know the way?

    I am the way, said the Lord.
    I am the way.
    Follow me.

    And she did.
    Alberta followed Him.
    Every step of the way.

    On down to Cincinnati
    where she now had grandchildren to love.

    She followed the Lord's call.
    She never lost faith.
    Willingly, wholeheartedly, she carried within her
    true concern
    for all the people God had given her
    to care for and pray for...
    friends and family whom she held in her heart
    with a gentleness and a joy
    that none of us
    will ever forget.

I have prepared a place for you, says the Lord.
Come inside!
    Enter this sacred door
    sprinkled with the Blood of the Lamb of God;
    step into the embrace of these arms of mine
    stretched out for you
    on the wood on the Cross;

    place your hand in mine,
    these hands of mine
    that shoved aside the stone
    rolled against the entrance of the tomb;
    the hands that broke the power of sin
    and the chains of death.

For I am Love. I am Love itself.

My love is patient. My love is kind.
It rejoices in the Truth.
It believes all things,
hopes all things.
endures all things.

Yes, love endures.
It endures all things.
Love never fails.

Welcome home, Bertie!
Welcome home!

A couple nights ago, I was at Leroy's house.
He and his son, Rob, were looking through old photograph albums.

Snapshots of tractors and backhoes
and collie dogs and Pontiacs;
graduations and weddings and baptisms.

I had other things to do,
but they kept pouring over the old photos,
laughing and reminiscing.

Later, after they had closed the covers
of those old photo albums,
I asked Rob which photographs
were the most memorable for him.

He thought a moment and said,
"The Christmases.
The family gatherings at Christmas time.
Those pictures capture it all."

"What do they capture?" I asked.

"Life," he said.
"This life is such a gift. It is such a wonderful gift."

What would it be like, I wonder,
to be able to capture…
in a few, chosen words,
in a few, vintage photographs,

> the essence of the Love that we all long for,
> the love that stirs deep within us
> each time we hear the word, *home,*
> that wonderful word, *home*?

The Bible tells us that God is love.
So, when you and I speak about love,
we are, in a sense, speaking about God.

> In a similar way, when we speak about *home,*
> are we not also speaking another name,
> articulating another name for God?

> The God who accompanies us throughout our life,
> from town to town, from house to house.

> In the good times and the hard times.
> In times of fulfillment, in times of confusion…
> always, Christ is at our side,
> reminding us: "I am the way, the truth, and the life."

> "Walk in my Truth," says the Lord.
> "Cherish my gift of Life.

> And *never* forget that *I am the Way.*
> *I am the way home.*

> No one comes to the Father but through me.
> And, in my Father's House, you will find…your *home.*
> Your *true* and *eternal home.*"

Made in the USA
Lexington, KY
06 November 2019